Dennis M. Wilson

The Cryptocurrency Mining Bible

By Dennis M. Wilson of CryptEdu.com a division of
Internetnextstep.com Consulting Ltd.

This Living Book v1.1 was Created on:

Thursday, August 31, 2017.

This Book is NOT FREE

Dennis M. Wilson

Contents

What is Crypto Currency?

Bitcoin, Ethereum, Litecoin, Dash, Ripple and many more, you have likely heard some of these names in the last 12 months. These are all examples of Crypto Currencies and they all operate on a decentralized computer network and software called the Blockchain.

Unlike traditional, "fiat" currencies like the USD, the Euro etc. which governments can arbitrarily increase the money supply and all transactions are centralized in the banking system, Cryptocurrencies are not centrally controlled and follow a firm set of rules put into existence at time of creation, and very difficult to change unless you get a majority buy in of the distributed network's computers and servers that contain the blockchain.

The blockchain essentially is the transaction ledger of all transactions and it eventually like in the case of Bitcoin or Ethereum exists on hundreds of thousands of computers and servers around the world.

Why?

Why would people keep this ledger on their servers and computers for free?

The simple answer is MINING!

What is Mining?

Well, as this is an entry level crypto currency course, we will keep it in very easy terms.

For the blockchain to operate, all transactions need to be verified by a certain number of nodes of the distributed network. This ensures nobody cheats and changes the ledger of their own node. If they did, the transaction would fail as it could be proven fraudulent as it would not be able to find 4 other machines randomly to verify it is real.

If you agree to host the "blockchain" on your computer, or on a "mining rig", the purpose is for you to solve a very complicated mathematical equation that is used in the secure verification process of each transaction. Confirmation of the transactions is paramount to the blockchain operating securely.

The reason people do the mining is the Block Reward. If you successfully mine a block, you get a reward. Currently the Bitcoin block reward is 12.5 coins, or at the time of this writing August 18, 2017, $4300 USD/Bitcoin x 12.5 = $53750!

This becomes very economical if the difficulty to mine costs less in electricity and crypto mining rig maintenance than the reward provides.

This is the essence of the blockchain, and why Crypto currency mining exists.

Mining

Since the advent of decentralization by way of Cryptographic digital currency utilizing the Blockchain in the year 2009, and the growing popularity of alternative cashless transactions in the global market, there is no denying that cryptocurrency is becoming more accepted as a legitimate mode of exchange for goods, services, and other commodities. Whether or not this form of digital currency could reach widespread circulation is not a question of probability but of time.

Data suggests a growing number of people getting involved both in the production of cryptocurrencies and its usage as can be seen with the increase in their circulating supply, volume, and relative value, as well as the proliferation of mining pools, mining contracts or services, mining architectures and mining hardware (mining 'rigs').

This is turning out to be especially true with secondary type currencies, also known as 'altcoins' because of the relative ease by which they can be mined compared to the primary, but more difficult to mine, 'bitcoin.'

Unlike traditional fiat money issued in banks, these crypto currencies will reach a supply limit (like 21 million BTC), at which point no additional units can be mined or added and their total number in circulation will become permanent. From a traditional standpoint, this makes such currency virtually resistant to inflation. However, nothing is set in stone when it comes to their current relative value as the rate of mining, 'minting', and coin-buying is, as of this moment, very dynamic and subject to a lot of internal and external factors.

Thus, venturing into the competitive and highly complex world of cryptocurrency mining requires a solid educational foundation about the ins and outs of this fledgling industry in order to make the most profitable investments in your mining method of choice.
It requires a basic understanding on how the blockchain mining system works, and some concepts about valuation and trading to guide you on which currency to bank your mining hardware and money on at any particular point in time. It is a very fluid industry and what made one person a fortune yesterday, can lose another a fortune today. Just like mining for gold and other precious gems or metals.

The Stakes of Becoming a Miner

The prospect of making a fortune with cryptocurrency mining is not a far-fetched idea. For instance, way back in 2010, bitcoins went largely unnoticed and unheard of, owing to its low value when converted to fiat currency and total lack of understanding coupled with perceived risk of getting involved. (10,000 BTC = 40 USD). Reportedly, one person used this currency to buy two pizzas with 10,000 BTC valued at 40 USD. Six years later, that value of those 10,000 bitcoins skyrocketed to more than 20 million USD.

Nowadays, more currencies are emerging, and some of them are starting to exhibit promises of increase in value relative to other currencies. As more people get involved and the processing power of mining technology improves, the possibility of striking the proverbial oil pit or gold mine may be just around the corner. It also may not be.

However, much like mining for real gold, there are stakes involved; you stand to lose money if you're not aware of the pros and cons of each method and the ability to make wise decisions on which currencies would be the most profitable ones to mine.

The cost of electricity and capital cost of your mining rig could easily cost more than the crypto currency you are mining, meaning you could lose all or part of your investment in mining rigs and electricity.

Choosing the Mining Method Best for YOU

Before mining became a widespread practice, people relied heavily on individual mining using their own hardware to calculate blocks of information on open source mining applications. These applications employ hash functions and specific algorithms to verify each block before they can be integrated into a blockchain, which is essentially a bunch of transactional data linked together into a series of encrypted information which can't be reasonably decrypted or altered.

However, as more and more blocks are mined and integrated into the blockchain, verifying each block becomes increasingly difficult to the point where a single miner, with his limited resources and processing power, cannot produce enough hash rate to verify bigger chunks of data and still make a profit from it.

This led to the creation of alternative mining methods such as rental contract mining, cloud mining services, mining pools, collocated mining facilities, and various combinations of these methods.

Without going into all the details on how each system works right now, we will begin by introducing you to the four most common ways to participate in this 'mining expedition' with or without your own dedicated crypto currency mining rig.

Cloud Mining

Signing up to cloud mining service is probably the easiest way to start earning crypto currencies. It doesn't require any hardware except your regular PC, laptop, or smartphone. You're essentially renting a tiny part of a large mining facility which runs all the calculations using state-of-the-art mining infrastructure and software.
They support multiple platforms and allow you to choose which currencies you wish to spend your money on.

However, it does involve some research especially when establishing the credibility of a certain cloud mining service. Furthermore, you need to be able to decide which currency would yield the most output before parting with your hard-earned money. In both instances, you'll benefit a lot from this method by making informed decisions instead of making random choices. Genesis Mining is one great example of a cloud mining service.

Solo Mining with PC or Mining Rig

This is likely the least effective way to participate in the crypto currency gold rush we see and hear around us. Fun as a hobby, yes. Actual return on investment in a reasonable time frame. Not likely.

While it is possible to do, there are a few significant drawbacks.

The first is your personal PC is not likely strong enough to earn a return after electricity unless you are mining an obscure Altcoin. Even then you would need to solve the equation yourself and get the entire block reward. The statistics on this happening with all but the newest and potentially valueless coins are not in your favor. You would be hoping to win a reward of a coin that one day skyrocketed in value as you would not earn a return after machine wear and tear and electricity cost in the short term.

Should you go with a mining rig, which can cost anywhere from $2000 to $6000 you "may" have enough hashpower to earn the reward on an altcoin all on your own, but it may take 6 months or a year to do so. Granted the reward would be potentially large, but will it be large enough to earn a profit?

You may want to consider a mining pool to increase your chances of earning with your own PC or a mining rig.

Mining Pools

Dennis M. Wilson

Joining a mining pool and participating in mining activity using your own computer is a more viable option (but not much due to limitations of your computers power and relative inefficiency when compared to a dedicated mining rig) if you want to earn a small income without having to spend thousands of dollars on a dedicated mining rig. It allows more control of your mining efforts compared to a cloud mining contract and has the potential of competing against large scale miners as it is effectively a huge amount of combined processing power consisting of all the miners who put their resources into the pool on a global scale.

Mining pools have a systematized way of rewarding each participant and it is different from one pool to another. Some examples include Pay-per-Share, Proportional, and Bitcoin Pooled mining. In any case, you will receive a portion of the reward commensurate to your contributed hashpower during the block solving process.

Another advantage of mining pools is you only have to pay a very small amount to join the pool and some even offer it for free and take a percentage of the reward. The only drawback is sometimes you have no way of telling if your own mining machine, in this case your PC or laptop, is performing well enough or is capable of handling the task when it comes to solving bigger blocks of data at a certain hash rate.

Joining a mining pool with your own mining rig is a very promising method to maximize your mining efforts because it allows you to have the best of both worlds. First, you'll be able to verify blocks much faster as a result of combining your processing power with all the other participants in the mining pool. Secondly, you'll have more flexibility and greater options for what coins to mine with your rig.

The Race is On

As years progress, more and more people will be competing in a mad dash to mine every single crypto currency until the final piece of every blockchain is solved. Fortunately, new crypto currencies hit the marketplace daily, and that rate is only likely to increase as the digital gold rush continues.

Hardware and software companies are now taking part in the arms race to produce faster, more powerful mining infrastructures, while on the other side of the battlefield are individual miners in mining pools, people joining forces in a combined effort to propagate the coin industry and earn their own piece of this revolution which is paving the way to a new era of inexpensive cashless transactions.

Start your journey by educating yourself about the benefits of adopting cryptocurrency in day to day transactions. Learn the basics on how to navigate the intricacies of mining and find the best possible outcomes in every situation by following certain rules and principles governing them. Mining, much like any other skill is acquired through patience and consistent effort.

Now let us get into a deep dive on the crypto currency mining concepts and methods we have just introduced to you.

Cloud Mining Services

Mining can be very daunting, especially for an absolute beginner. Even if you have your own resources or the capability to mine on your own, you still must understand a lot of factors which can drastically affect your mining efforts. The smartest way forward may be to employ the services of expert miners who possess all the technical know-how of cryptocurrency mining, state-of-the-art mining facilities, and years of providing reliable mining services to clients.

Cloud mining services offer a quick solution to ordinary people who want to participate in cryptocurrency mining and be able to earn income without spending hundreds of dollars on mining rigs and computing hardware. It eliminates the problem of having to be responsible for excessive monthly bills on electricity and mining rig maintenance, not to mention dealing with the heat and noise of the physical rigs if you are trying to do it in your basement.

Not surprisingly, it is the method of choice of over 500,000 subscribers worldwide to a single cloud mining service, and there are more than 1.

To get you started, we need to understand many interrelated factors that will determine how much you can potentially earn after taking all aspects of the mining process into consideration. However, before venturing into any kind of cloud mining service, be sure to verify the credibility of the cloud mining company. Are they legit? Are they consolidators or resellers? Do they exist as a physical mining operation somewhere? (some pseudo-mining companies are nothing more than sophisticated Ponzi schemes).

The Real Cost of Mining

Mining costs money. Beyond the cost of setting up your own rig powerful enough to compete with other miners on a global network which means buying expensive hardware and running it at full speed 24 hours a day, seven days a week. Operational costs with the biggest one being the cost of electricity where your mining rig is located would depend on the type of mining equipment being used and maintaining the best possible conditions for the rig.

A custom-built DIY rig which use multiple GPUs (6) running at 25 to 50 mega hashes per second (MH/s) would consume around 400 to 800 watts. Let us say we have 800 watts running for an hour, this would be .8kwh of electricity, and an average rate in North America per kwh is $0.10. So just running the rig for 1 hour would cost 8 cents in electricity, or just over $57/month.

ASICs, on the other hand, are much more efficient because they are manufactured for mining purposes from the ground up. If you are looking to mine bitcoin you would need an Antminer S9, they consume 1328 watts. It would cost just over $99/month for most people to run this mining rig. Either way, you'll have to deal with these electricity bills mining any of these crypto currency coins.
The goal of course if find a coin or coins that mine at a rate that is profitable after you look at your machine cost and your electricity and maintenance costs.

Aside from having a reputation as energy guzzlers, mining rigs also require optimal working conditions to make sure they're running at full capacity and efficiency. Since mining rigs need to fire on all cylinders, you need an efficient cooling system and backup power to prevent a catastrophic meltdown. This means an additional cost on top of the electricity bills for running your rig.

The initial startup and the maintenance cost are just one piece of the puzzle. You must also understand the availability of various coins on the global network and the increasing level of difficulty for them to be mined. If the price of the coin you are mining does not go up in value at least as fast as the difficulty to mine it does, you will find your mining operation becoming less and less profitable as time goes on. Your hashpower essentially degrades over time in this scenario meaning it will eventually become NOT profitable to mine that particular coin in those particular market conditions. It doesn't mean all is lost, but it may mean you need to find another coin, or unplug your rigs until conditions become more favorable.

The downside to this is the new machines entering the market are more and more powerful than your old rig now collecting dust waiting for the right timing to re-enter the market.

Once you understand these principals, you start to grasp what crypto currency miners could realistically earn with their mining equipment.

For some currencies, it could take days or weeks to solve even just one block of data using high-end DIY rigs, while some newer currencies could only take a few hours. Their values will vary from one currency to another, and miners will have to decide which currencies they'll spend their money on at a given time.

As a general rule, if the overall cost of mining a certain currency exceeds the value and quantity of mined coins, i.e., 'rewards,' mining becomes unprofitable. They should either upgrade their mining speeds to meet the required hash rates, or switch to newer, low-priced alternative currencies with their lower hash rates and slightly different hash algorithms.

There is quite a large risk and high level of knowledge required to run your own rigs. This is why cloud mining services were born.

Buying a Cloud Mining Contract

As a cloud mining subscriber, you can earn your first coins and not worry about anything except paying the contract price of a particular mining service and choosing the right currency. However, it's good to understand what these companies are constantly going through to provide these services to regular people. This allows us to appreciate every bit of profit we earn instead of complaining about the maintenance fees the cloud mining companies take to do it all for you.

There are 3 types of mining contracts available today: **Co-location Hosted Mining, and Cloud Based Mining, and Leased or Rented hashing power.**

Co-Location Hosted Mining

This is paying a company for space in their rack in their data center to "host" YOUR mining rig or rigs. You would be in control of what mining pool to connect it to and what coins etc. to mine just as if it were in your basement, but it is NOT in your basement. You will pay a fee monthly for the mining rig's space in the rack and the electricity it uses. Often these mining rig co-location facilities also offer a maintenance contract so the co-location facility will monitor and maintain your rigs for you for an additional fee PLUS any parts needing replacement.

Cloud Based Mining

Cloud based mining is even simpler and very often novice miner's entry into crypto currency mining due to its simplicity and some would argue lessened risk. There are some massive Cloud Mining operations in the world today, some of which have over 500,000 individual subscribers.

Dennis M. Wilson

The Cloud Based Mining company procures, provisions, and maintains all the equipment. You are essentially just "allocated" your purchased amount of hashpower.

You will pay a fee upfront based upon how much hashpower you wish to purchase. This is often similar in cost, though sometimes cheaper than buying a rig at retail yourself with the same hashpower.

Cloud mining services don't lease specific mining units, but instead allocates a certain hash rate for you based on your chosen contract price. You can think of it like subscribing to an Internet service provider in which you pay for the internet speed. The higher your hash rate, the better the chances of earning. They mine specific currencies and let you choose which currency to mine and at what hash rate.

Payouts are given after reaching the threshold where your portion of the block reward exceeds the cost to power and maintain the equipment you have bought a slice of. Normally, it would take six months to about a year before you have earned your initial investment back and start to see profit. From that point onwards, you'll start earning positive income and see the real benefits of subscribing to a cloud mining service.

There seem to be 2 different kinds of contracts available from various mining companies.

Lifetime Contracts
Lifetime contracts seem to revolve around Bitcoin most of the time. It seems most altcoin contracts are time limited.

This sounds amazing, right? Pay once, earn money FOREVER? Yes, it certainly does get marketed that way, but the reality is much more realistic, yet still better than conventional ways to earn money.

The reality is, your hashpower will degrade over time due to increasing difficulty to mine the coin, as well as newer equipment being more efficient for the same operational cost. This ultimately leads you to earning a smaller and smaller reward after your electricity and maintenance costs are paid unless a few things work in your favor. Should the value of the coin your mining contract mines go up in value faster than the difficulty to mine it increases, you could technically keep earning for years. It is more realistic to realize your return will likely stop or become insignificant within 3 years or so in reasonable market conditions.

With all Cloud Mining Contracts, they can also be cancelled. This means there is RISK. With some Cloud Mining companies, if your mining profit is not more than your maintenance fees for only 3 consecutive days, the contract will be cancelled. The more reputable companies give 30 or 60 days of non-profitability before cancelling the contract.

The Internet is loaded with angry stories by people who chased a higher reward on a coin called Litecoin as it was billed as the most profitable coin to mine. Sadly a few cloud mining companies started offering contracts to mine this coin. The coin difficulty SPIKED and the price TANKED, and everybody had their contracts voided.

The sad part is, if they would have gone with the steady return coins, they wouldn't have lost, they chose to chase the HIGH RISK HIGH REWARD coin and lost. Sadly, they then took to the internet en-masse complaining and calling the cloud mining company a scam. We hope this Crypto Currency Mining course will give you enough knowledge to understand what you are getting into and realize the truth is GOOD ENOUGH when it comes to cloud mining contracts.

Please note, Ethereum cloud mining contracts could end up with an abrupt end to mining profits should the long planned Proof of Work (POW) method of transaction validation turn to the Proof of Stake (POS) which is planned to start happening in November of 2017, possibly starting as a merged method until full adoption.

This will SIGNIFICANTLY affect Ethereum mining contracts profitability.

Most of the major cloud mining companies are promising to do their best to redirect the mining power to other altcoins, but there are no promises they will be the same profitability.

Time Limited Contracts

Many of the Cloud Mining Companies offer time limited terms like 2 years or 1000 days vs. open lifetime contracts. It is not clear as to why they do not offer lifetime contracts on these altcoins other than most contacts in normal conditions would naturally be almost done for profitability at this point unless a dramatic rise in coin value continued to outpace mining difficulty.

Leased or Rented Hashing Power

This is a slight variation on buying a contract in a large cloud mining operation. This is you renting actual hashpower for a set period of time from another person who is willing to rent out their mining power. This could be an individual with a single mining rig that he is willing to rent out for 8 hours a day to someone else. There are a few websites that facilitate this type of cloud based mining..

An advantage of this is you can test particular mining rigs against particular currencies and mining pools to learn the best way for you to invest your money into either a formal cloud based mining contract or actual equipment purchase.

Currency and Hash Rates

Cryptocurrencies are in a constant state of flux. There's no telling when a certain currency will experience a drop or increase in value, although it's pretty sure they are getting harder and taking longer to mine. There are several factors that can contribute to the profitability of mining a certain kind of currency.

Current Value – Cryptocurrencies, like precious metals, are valued based on certain principles in economics, the time and resources expended in maintaining the blockchain's security and integrity, blockchain difficulty, and even more importantly, public perception. In general, currencies with a low supply and high demand are of higher value. They are sought after and used by more people, hence they are constantly low in supply and are priced higher. From a miner's standpoint, these currencies are the most difficult ones to mine because they require higher hash rates as more people get involved.

Hash Rates – How fast a mining rig can solve, i.e. guess the lowest hash code to be used by the system for the next block in the blockchain depends on its 'hash rate.' They are measured in megahash per second (MH/s), gigahash per second (GH/s), terahash per second (TH/s), petahash per second (PH/s), and so on. Basically, the miner tries to guess a random number (nonce) which is fed into the hash algorithm (e.g. SHA 256) such that it would result in a hash code lower than the previous block. It goes through millions or trillions of iterations every second (hence the term 'hash per second') until it finally gets the desired hash code. Every iteration, the mining rig burns energy which shows itself in monthly electricity and cooling bills. Certain currencies use hash algorithms that put a lot of burden on the mining rigs and this only gets worse as more currencies are added to the eco-system. On the other hand, some cryptocurrencies are starting to adopt more secure yet efficient hashing algorithms to take the weight off the mining rigs by allowing lower hash rates.

It's important to note being involved in crypto currency mining requires your participation. Even if you have started seeing gains on a particular currency in the first six months, it doesn't mean it will continue to gain at the same rate in the coming months. It is true, in the past some people have lost their contracts because the slow rate of production ate up their cloud mining company's resources to the point of the contract no longer being profitable. This usually happens if the hash rates for a certain currency have already increased, or the demand or price of that currency has already dropped.

The solution? Always keep track of your mining efforts. Monitor your gains and watch for signs of opportunity by mining other cryptocurrencies with your hashpower. It does involve a certain amount of luck, but at least we are able to make calculated risks and not rely on luck alone.

Mining Pools Using Laptops and PCs

Mining pools provide a safe and easy way for cryptocurrency miners to keep track of their own progress in collaborative mining, and yield sufficient profit from the mining hardware they own. This section refers to simply your laptops or personal computers. This method is highly favored by a large majority of hobby currency miners all over the world for several reasons.

First, it doesn't require insanely huge amounts of computing power. Way back in 2008, cryptocurrencies, like Bitcoin, could still be feasibly mined in any household computer. Today, you need 2830 terahash per second to make a single Bitcoin! Even the best laptops and PCs can no longer keep up mining major currencies such as Bitcoin and Ethereum.

Mining can still be barely profitable in mining pools when mining minor coins ('altcoins') such as Monero, Dash, and Dogecoin (keep in mind which are possible and profitable is constantly changing so make sure you refer to the publish date on this document to see how recent it is) using no other mining equipment except your trusty laptop or PC. Gaming machines with great video cards will work considerably better for mining altcoins.

Mining pools can have hundreds, or even thousands of miners contributing their computer power to solve blocks of transactions simultaneously. Eventually, a lucky miner will stumble on the solution, after which the pool would split the reward among all the members based on their contributed hashpower. This is a considerable advantage over solo mining where miner's machines try to guess the right combination individually, and earn absolutely nothing until they are finally successful. It is hardly even possible for laptops and PC to do this anymore.

Mining pools with a good PC or gaming machine can provide a trickle of stable income with less upfront cost as you are employing a machine you already own. They won't be able to give you the same return as solo dedicated rig or cloud contract mining, but the steady flow of bits and pieces accrued from these rewards could provide you with a decent residual income over time.

Striking it rich don't usually happen in mining pools because it doesn't reward people based on who got the right hash code. Your pay would depend on how much work you were able to contribute to the pool. The higher the hash rates your laptop or PC have, the bigger your share compared to others.

Another advantage of mining pools is that it doesn't involve a lot of money to start generating a very tiny residual income. You're basically using the same piece of equipment you've already own, or maybe doing just a few upgrades like buying a couple of GPUs and extra RAM to boost your hash rates.

Gaming laptops and PCs are usually built with high-end GPUs (Graphics Processing Unit) to handle graphics. When mining minor Altcoin currencies, we could use our machines containing high-end GPU's to perform the required mathematical computations at higher speeds. Fees for joining mining pools are almost negligible; some even offer them for free. In other words, you've got nothing to lose except the electricity.

A downside to trying to mine Altcoins from your laptop of gaming machine is it is VERY hard to know if you are turning a profit or not as you do not truly know how much your electricity bill is going up as a result of you mining coins. After you have done it for a few months you will know, but if you are losing, it will be too late as your losses will be crystalized.

Choosing Your Mining Pool

After realizing the potential of mining pools to the whole mining industry, mining pools began to grow in size and number. Mining pools allow people from around the world to band together and 'pool' their resources in the form of raw computing power. This allows them to compete with large scale miners with the most basic mining tools used to collectively produce the massive hash rates necessary for mining minor currencies.

However, not all mining pools offer the same capabilities and most have different reward structures. This means, your potential income would also depend on the mining pools themselves you chose to join, in addition to your laptop or PC's maximum hash rates. You may be able to earn a small amount of residual income going for minor currencies because they require less computing power. With major currencies like Bitcoin and Ethereum, chances of earning a reward are very slim, and your potential earnings using your own laptop or PC are negligible to non-existent so likely not even worth considering.

Dennis M. Wilson

Take note of the following properties when choosing your mining pool:

Pool Size

Generally speaking, bigger pools are better and faster at solving blocks compared to smaller ones. The reason is obvious; there are more people trying to 'guess' the right hash code compared to a small mining pool. However, if we're going to consider the hash rates of individual miners joining the pool, we might have a completely different picture.

A small mining pool consisting of miners that use high-end, dedicated mining hardware could outpace a bigger one with thousands of miners who only have their laptops and PCs running as mining equipment. Ultimately, it comes down to the combined hash rate generated by the entire pool. Currently, Antpool holds the biggest in terms of hash rate at 23.1 percent of the world's total mining capability, followed by BTC.TOP at 12 percent, BTC.com at 7.6 percent, F2Pool at 6.9 percent, BTCC Pool at 6.6 percent, and BW.COM at 5.4 percent. (Note: these values are updated daily at:

https://blockchain.info/pools

Hence, these numbers may no longer reflect the current values at the time of reading.)

Reward Structure

Depending on your computer's mining capability, mining schedule, and preferred payout frequency, you may choose a mining pool with a different reward structure rather than the usual proportional reward-to-contributed work scheme. For instance, a Pay Per Share (PPS) structure allows you to earn rewards based on your share of the probability, and hence the difficulty, of solving the block which you've contributed to pool, and be able to earn them without having to wait for a complete solve. Compare this to a Proportional (PROP) reward structure where you are paid for your hash rate regardless of the difficulty or share of the actual number of hash codes you were able to generate. PPS has a more stable payout but would also exact higher fees to miners, while a PROP payout would depend on how well or how fast the entire pool was able to solve the block and usually has lower fees.

Currencies

Some mine pools specialize on a certain kind of cryptocurrency which require a minimum hash rate to become profitable. A mid-range laptop or PC is way better at mining minor, relatively low-priced cryptocurrencies because they would usually require lower hash rates. As a rule, the greater the number of people trying to mine a certain currency, the more hash rate it would require for each individual miner. Most cryptocurrency systems will try to raise the level of difficulty of the next block relative to the speed the previous block has been solved. As a result, only a certain amount of block can be solved at a given time. It's a safety feature in most cryptocurrencies to preclude the possibility of double-spending or 51 percent attacks which would eventually lead to a currency being totally wiped out. Hence, the harder for a certain currency to mine, the more secure it becomes and vice versa.

Bear in mind with each mining pool, there will be a trade-off between your pay structure, with their corresponding fees, and the kind of mining hardware you use. It's typically a very low-yield investment to try to mine with a laptop or home computer in a pool and is mostly suited to hobbyist types or kids living at home that do not pay for electricity.

The crypto currency you choose to mine is also a factor. Since you are not risking much other than some minorly increased electricity bills with this method of hobby mining, it's may even yield more than just letting your money sit in the bank at today's interest rates barely worth mentioning.

Mine Individually with Your Mining Rigs

Buying or building your own rig for your solo mining efforts should only be attempted if you are already relatively experienced with mining and have a deeper understanding of how to properly run and configure your mining rig. Otherwise, your whole system could fail and you end up losing a reasonable sum of money in the process.

The most prevalent issues with running your own rig, aside from the initial cost and electricity bills, are the maintenance and proper ventilation to keep it running. For solo miners, it's a tough balancing act between processing power and keeping the temperature down.

Often things go great for 4 to 6 months and you think it is easy. Then things start to wear out and breakdown. Computers running at this intensity have chips fail, fans fail, connectors melt or fail. It is a constant maintenance issue once you pass the 4 to 6-month mark.

Most of the time, it's going to require an ASIC (application-specific integrated circuit) or more to be able to generate a profit since most GPUs and PCs can't run the calculations fast enough for bigger blocks of information. It usually mines high value currencies like bitcoin and Ethereum because of its raw power, although the same ASIC can be used to mine other currencies such as Litecoin and Dash.

Dedicated mining rigs make up most of the computing power currently in cryptocurrency mining. They are the backbone of the mining industry because of their unique ability to perform countless calculations at incredible speeds.

A single ASIC mining rig with its 14 TH/s processors can outperform a pool of a hundred PCs or laptops with 20 GH/s GPUs each. Cloud mining facilities and mining farms have thousands of specialized mining rigs. If 14 TH/s is not staggering enough for just one mining rig, imagine a warehouse full of them firing on all cylinders.

Incredible mining ability comes at a heavy price. It is strongly recommended to weigh the facts carefully before investing in a mining rig or building one yourself. Individual or solo mining is probably the most expensive way to mine cryptocurrencies nowadays.

Because of the potential to yield higher returns compared to other methods, and because it gives miners full control of the mining equipment, mining software, and running cost, people still consider them as a viable mining option.

Before entertaining the thought of buying a mining rig, consider the following factors in cryptocurrency mining business.

Type of Currency

Bitcoin and Ethereum are the two major currencies being used the most by people worldwide. They're also the highest in terms of relative value which makes them very attractive for miners. Sadly, mining these currencies also means competing with millions of other miners worldwide hoping to best each other in solving one block at a time.

Bitcoin, for instance has already peaked at more than 1,000,000,000 billion hashes per second (EH/s) for the entire network of Bitcoin miners. This would literally make your solitary ASIC miner a drop in the ocean and it would statistically take around 12 years to solve one block of transaction and even that would take some good luck. With Ethereum, your odds are a little higher at around 50 to 70 TH/s. Even then one ASIC miner won't do much better, you probably need five or more to make a real profit.

Mining for minor currencies or altcoins (e.g., Dash, Litecoin, and Monero) is a better option because they don't require extremely high number of hashes per second and the difficulty is not that high as well. They also use different hash algorithms (e.g., Scrypt, X11, and Cryptonight) which could be more efficient in electricity consumption than the older SHA 256 used by the Bitcoin blockchain.

Here's a caveat for mining altcoins: not too many people are using them at the moment and their relative value is quite low. Nonetheless, your mining rig gives you an unfair advantage over many other altcoin miners who don't have a dedicated rig, which can lead to higher overall profitability in altcoins.

Electricity Cost

The cost of buying a mining rig or possibly housing a roomful of mining rigs (mini-farm) is only part of the total annual cost of mining cryptocurrency. You need power to run the mining rigs. With just one ASIC mining rig running at 1.6 kW/h non-stop, depending on your electricity cost, you're going to spend around 5 dollars a day or 150 dollars a month. As you are going it alone in cryptocurrency mining in this scenario, you will probably need more than one mining rig to get realistic returns.

Suppose you need five rigs for a certain currency requiring 70 TH/s to solve one block. At 15 cents per kW/h, five 14 TH/s-rigs (70 TH/s total) running at 1.6 kW/h apiece translates to 28.8 dollars a day or 864 dollars a month in electricity bills. Again, this would depend on the electricity cost of the country and possibly even city you live in. If you plan on setting up a 'mini-farm', you'll have to add the cost of running the cooling systems on top of your electricity bills for running the rigs, in order to keep them working in optimal conditions and producing their highest possibly hash rates. The warmer your chips run, the less hash rate they produce.

Major currencies require higher hash rates, and thus higher consumption of electricity. For instance, the power consumption for Bitcoin mining nowadays is high enough to light up a small city. When going solo on Bitcoin with its ridiculously huge hash rates, your electricity bills could reach astronomical proportions. With altcoins, however, you could actually make more money from every kilowatt you consume with your mining rig. Always check the dollar value per altcoin to see if you're making gains and can expect a return on your investment mining that particular currency at that point in time. Things are constantly changing as far as the most profitable coin to mine day to day.

Some pools have some great automated features that automatically switch to the most profitable coin at any given time and auto convert the reward to your desired currency.

Profit

Buying mining rigs is more like buying a franchise to open a shop; you can't expect a return on your investment in a few days or without studying the business model a bit. On average, it could take a year or more, depending on your mining rigs' capabilities.

Certain factors to be considered when trying to project the profitability of cryptocurrency mining as a single mining entity includes initial startup cost, operational and maintenance costs, and cryptocurrency to fiat currency value. You can find online profitability calculators such as https://www.coinwarz.com/calculators to compute your estimated profit for mining a certain currency.

Most calculators do not account for solo mining and computations are based mainly on partial rewards for solving a block of transaction in a pool. As mentioned earlier, it would take you 12 years to mine a single Bitcoin as an individual miner, assuming the level of difficulty and hash rate requirement doesn't change much and you are pretty good at winning lotteries.

For altcoins, you will have a better chance to be the first one to solve each block with a high-end mining rig. Check the dollar value of your mined altcoins. If your monthly income is greater than your electricity bills, then you're gaining something from it. But you're not into any profit just yet. First you need to get your capital investment back, THEN you will start to profit.

For example, let us say you bought a 14TH/s-mining rig at $3,000 and you're trying to mine an altcoin worth $50 each. Since you're a 'big guy' with such a powerful mining rig, let us pretend you could mine 10 of these altcoins per month, worth $500. At 12 cents per kW/h, and your mining rig running at full speed 24/7, you'll pay approximately $138 dollars for the electricity bills. This means you would earn a $362 on top of your electricity rates.

Assuming the price of the altcoin and its hash rate remain stable, in just 8 and a half months, you will have earned back your capital investment, and from here on out, you'll start seeing the return on your mining rig investment.

The story doesn't end there. As your chosen altcoin expands and gains popularity, the difficulty and hash rate requirement would also increase, necessitating the purchase of yet another, or perhaps even more powerful, mining rig to keep up your returns, unless that altcoin goes up substantially in value.

Nothing Ventured, Nothing Gained

These numbers aren't meant to discourage you from doing solo mining with the kind of mining hardware you plan to have. This is just to point out that with every method, there would be a risk/reward relationship – the higher the risk, the greater the rewards.

There is no room for half-measures in solo mining; it's an all-out arms race with millions of other miners who are trying to best each other for mining supremacy and maximum financial reward.

You don't want to waste your time and money on something without have a fighting chance to win. What good is a 20 GH/s-mining rig if you have plenty others competing with you with 30 GH/s mining rigs? Absolutely nothing. You need to put everything you got into this method to get results.

We recommend joining a pool vs. going it alone.

Joining Pools with Your Own Mining Rigs

Buying your own ASIC or building your own GPU mining rig and plugging it into a mining pool is arguably the most lucrative method of cryptocurrency mining. It's a compromise between two extremes.

Pool mining using your own PC or laptop provides a low-risk, low-income option for miners on a budget who just want to learn and experiment.
Solo mining allows for high-risk, high-yield investment for miners who can afford expensive mining rigs, cooling systems, and all related expenses of cryptocurrency mining.

Cloud mining contracts land somewhere in the middle. Your returns are not as good as you give up a portion of your mining reward to the cloud mining company as a daily maintenance fee.

Dennis M. Wilson

Joining a mining pool and directing your mining rig hashpower to is almost the best of both worlds, namely:

- ❏ reduced variance (degree of uncertainty) in finding the right hash through the combined computing power of the entire pool

- ❏ increased income potential as you get paid full value for the quality of your contributed mining rig hashpower.

Nothing is set in stone when it comes to the actual income of pool miners who use specialized ASIC mining rigs or DIY GPU mining units. There are many instances where buying your own mining rig and plugging in to a mining pool is the most advantageous in cryptocurrency mining.

Several factors come into play when computing the profitability of joining a certain pool, such as pool fees, the reward scheme, the kind of mining hardware you have, the cost of electricity for running it, the dollar value of the currency you're mining, and how big is the pool. Does it have enough hash rate resources including yours to actually solve blocks?

Your Mining Rig and the Pool Size

Joining large pools is the norm in pool mining for obvious reasons. Large pools tend to find more blocks at a faster rate compared to smaller ones. Broadly speaking, a pool's aggregate hashpower and ability to mine currencies is related to, or is directly proportional to the size of its combined hashpower.

Since the whole mining business is based on probability, we can't exactly tell how many blocks a large pool can mine at a given time (although the variance in finding a block for bigger pools are much smaller).

A pool can have tens of thousands of low-end miners who use their home computers and laptops, or maybe just a few hundred who use high-end GPU or ASIC miners, or everything in between. Regardless of each participant's mining capability, it all comes down to the combined hash rate of the entire pool.

So how does pool size affect your potential earnings? For the sake of illustration, we will use the proportional reward scheme. In large pools, you can expect smaller, albeit more stable income for its enormous hash rate and low variance.

Using the proportional reward scheme, your pay will be based on how much work (number of hashes) you were able to contribute to the pool in solving a particular block relative to all the other miners in that pool. It doesn't consider who got the right hash.

Hence, if your work amounts to 0.01% of the total work done by the entire pool in solving a particular block for that round, and the reward for solving such block is 10 units, you will get 0.01 units.

However, being big doesn't necessarily mean you can take the credit for solving a block every single time. Again, this is all about probability, and your mining rigs guess is just as good as everybody else's.

Dennis M. Wilson

Your Mining Rig and the Pool's Reward Scheme

Pools have different ways of rewarding miners for their work. Depending on your hardware's capabilities, you may go for Pay per Share (PPS), Pay per Last N Shares (PPLNS), and Proportional (PROP).

Pay per Share (PPS)

Rewards miners based on the amount of work they've done. However, it's not just any kind of work. The reward system uses a 'gold standard' – in this case the level of difficulty tied to a certain currency against all the hashes submitted by individual miners are evaluated. Thus, only those who were able to submit work based on a given difficulty will get their payouts.

The advantage of PPS over other reward schemes is that it doesn't require a solved block per round, and miners will get a fixed rate based on the difficulty they are willing to commit to solve a particular block. This is where individual mining prowess becomes a dominant factor in pool mining because it favors miners who can generate significant number of hashes that has a certain property.

PPS pools pays out its miners on a regular basis whether or not a block was found by the pool. This puts the pool at risk of losing money. To stay in business, they charge higher fees compared to other payout schemes (as much as 7.5% to 10% in some pools). Small-time miners and hobbyists will have a difficult time breaking even, especially if they're mining capabilities are severely limited. Power miners with their more robust ASICs and GPUs can take advantage of this payout scheme.

Proportional (PROP)

This reward scheme is used in most 'free-for-all' mining pools because it doesn't place the pool manager at risk; the miners are. The reason for this is pretty obvious – no solved block, no reward for the entire pool on that particular round. Regardless of the difficulty and the number of hashes your mining rig was able to come up it all goes out the window if your pool loses that round.

On the other hand, if your pool happens to win that round, you as a pool miner will reap the benefits of contributing so much in finding the right hash. It doesn't have to be you specifically; it can be anyone else in the pool, perhaps even some small-time miner who just happened to get lucky. The great thing about this is you would actually earn more than the lucky guy who accidentally found it. This can happen in a pool since all of you are basically just guessing the answer.

As mentioned earlier, there would be some kind of 'trade-off' between the size of the pool and your potential income in this kind of reward system. It would take some experimenting to find the delicate balance between the two. Too large of a pool will diminish your mining rig's 'speed advantage'; too small will put you at risk of not finding any block at all, in exchange for greater rewards.

Pay per Last N Shares (PPLNS)

This is somewhat similar to PROP except it still accounts for your last shares in previous rounds where the pool failed to find the right hash, and rewards them to you when a new block is solved. Unlike PROP where everything restarts every round, your efforts that came close to the valid hash won't be thrown away by the system after a lost round, but would still be considered for payouts when a solved block comes around.

Choosing the Right Mining Rigs for Pool Mining

By this time, you may already have an idea which rig you want to buy or which pool to join. Solo mining in a pool is not recommended for beginners because there are a lot of moving parts to deal with initially. As you gain more experience, you may try investing in a mining rig and attach it to a pool and work yourself towards world domination slowly but surely.

How to Maximize Profits with Cloud Mining

More people are getting into cloud mining as solo mining becomes less and less profitable for small-time miners. The cost of owning high-end mining rigs that are 'mine-worthy' by today's hash standards are extremely high, not to mention expensive to run and maintain. They also rapidly depreciate newer faster mining rigs or GPU's hit the market given new entrants an advantage over you with a 2-year-old mining rig.

This results in diminishing returns in a relatively short period of time. This is especially true when mining major currencies like Bitcoin and Ethereum.

Consequently, even large mining companies are forced to replace older mining rigs with newer, more powerful yet energy-efficient rigs just to stay in business. Some go so far as selling their old mining rigs to potential buyers who might be interested in pool mining as more superior versions of the old rigs become available to the market.

The key to cloud mining's popularity is the relative ease people can mine cryptocurrencies using nothing more than their mobile devices, online wallet, internet connection, and mining fees. Some cloud mining sites even have auto features allowing miners to alternate between pools and currencies or trade their altcoins from one currency to another automatically.

What Profit to Expect?

The biggest issue with Cloud based mining is people go into it with unrealistic expectations of profit.

Earnings with cloud mining often come in small increments and break even somewhere between 6 to 18 months as long as the coin value doesn't drop and the difficulty increase to the point the contract gets cancelled due to non-profitability. Not all cloud mining companies are the same. Some sites exact smaller fees per gigahash while their maintenance fees may be a bit more expensive or vice versa. To maximize profits in cloud mining, research and 'gut instinct' are two of your best allies.

Cryptocurrency Cloud Mining is Risky

For some reason people on the internet have decided you are supposed to get your investment back in days, weeks, or months at NO risk. If you believe this, we have seen some great Florida "beachfront property" for sale on the internet for super cheap you and those who believe fast, fully secured contracts with big returns exist in Crypto Cloud Mining may want to look at.

Cloud Mining should be compared to the return possible on buying and maintaining your OWN mining rig. It is a way to participate in cloud mining WITHOUT needing to purchase rapidly depreciating equipment. Equipment that depreciates both in physical condition causing constant maintenance and parts replacement, and the ability to earn a reward due to a reward split, OR degradation of hashpower as a result of difficulty constantly increasing.

The perfect storm for LONG TERM mining returns is a coin that goes up in value over time FASTER than the difficulty increase degrades hashpower. This allows for the maintenance fee which includes depreciation of machines, maintenance and repair, electricity, and staffing to always leave you with a profit margin.

It is also important to note that many complain about how the cloud mining company takes this daily FEE in real USD to cover its cost and be profitable. This EXACT thing happens in the mutual fund world, it is called a management fee. Your mutual fund crashes and kills off 50% of your retirement savings, and guess what, yep you got it, they STILL TAKE THEIR

Dennis M. Wilson

MANAGEMENT fee. What a bunch of scammers right?!

Should the perfect mining storm of you mining a coin that goes up in value the same or faster than the difficulty to mine it not happen for you, BEWARE, your contract can be cancelled as it becomes NO LONGER profitable to run the mining rig on your behalf.

This is one of the BIGGEST risks of being involved in Crypto Currency Mining with any cloud mining company.

This does NOT make crypto mining a scam, it is the reality of how it works, and the risk you accept by purchasing a mining contract with any cloud mining provider.

Let us be CLEAR.

Do Your Research!

Know you are NOT looking to get your money back in 2 weeks or even 6 months in many cases. Know if the coin you are mining's value goes down in value FASTER than the difficulty to mine it, YOU MAY END UP WITH YOUR CONTRACT CANCELLED. NO REFUNDS, not partial money back.

This is IDENTICAL to if you owned your own mining rig.

Many on the internet have said, "at least if I own my own mining rig vs. a cloud mining contract, I could always choose to sell it if things became unprofitable." Really? So you would be the only one who found out it is not profitable and could sell your rig or its GPU's? For how much? ummmmm. ZERO or close to it comes to mind as the market would be FLOODED with those who had the same thought.

Be careful in chasing a mining contract on the latest FAD coin. Many reddit complainers got caught up in chasing a goldrush with a coin that did awesome out of the gate then crashed and became unprofitable very quickly. They relentlessly blamed the particular cloud mining company for scamming them. If they had NOT picked such a risky coin, they may have done better. They chased the FAST Reward and LOST. It happens in the fully regulated stock market EVERY DAY, yet nobody says the Stock Market is a scam. The worst part is, it was those same purchasers that relentlessly pushed the cloud mining company to sell contracts for that particular coin!

We believe in the Truth of Cloud mining, as we believe the truth is good enough.

Cloud Mining vs. Real World Mutual Funds

If you put $2000 into a savings account paying 3% annual interest compounding monthly, how much money would you have in 1 year? At 1 year, you would have $2060.83, at 2 years you would have $2123.51.

What if you got a 10% annual return compounded monthly? Mutual funds have achieved this lately but the last time they hit these returns over a period of time, a serious correction wiped out as much as 1/2 of the average person's retirement savings as we were in a BUBBLE.

Some think we are once again in a bubble. Your return on a 10% mutual fund would be 1 year $2,209.43, 2 years $2,440.78.

These are REAL WORLD INVESTMENT returns that average people get excited about EVERY day.

Let us look at a potential scenario in cloud mining for Bitcoin. I will let you replicate this with the available calculators etc. We ran some extensive numbers against returns from July and August of 2017 with a reputable mining company. We made some assumptions to try to keep this as real as possible.

These numbers are based upon the assumption difficulty will increase by .37% compounding daily, so returns will diminish to zero and the contract would be cancelled over time eventually IF the price of Bitcoin does NOT go up to offset difficulty and keep the mining contract profitable. We are using a Bitcoin price of $3347.27 and NOT assuming it goes up in value over the time frame. Many think this is impossible, but lets try to look seriously at this as with the current spike in Bitcoin value, it has made a lot of lifetime Bitcoin Cloud mining contract holders VERY happy as their returns suddenly jumped a LOT.

This is also based upon the reward of 12.5 coins, which of course without a massive spike in value of bitcoin on or before the next halving to 6.25 coins, which according to http://www.bitcoinblockhalf.com at the time of this writing is expected 17 Jun 2020, your contract could die on this day.

Expected return even with these restrictions, in 1 year $2,598.60, in two years $3,293.64. We show the contract finally dying due to non-profitability after 2914 days with total money earned of $3,531.37 We saw payback of original contract price in 207 days, yes that is MORE than 6 months! Imagine if you kept your earnings in Bitcoin as well and it continued to go up in value? This example is selling it for cash as soon as you are paid it.

Back to the real world, this is about 8 years before it died. Of course, it is possible this contract would die on June 17, 2020 with the halving depending on Bitcoin's value at that time.

What would our investment in a real world mutual fund be in the same time frame?

Regular money market fund/savings at 3%: $2541.74
Regular mutual fund at 10%: $4436.35

From 1992–2011, the S&P's average is 9.07% that is 17 years that we wouldn't have even hit our 10% guess. In 2011, it was -1.12%, you would have LOST ground.

From 1987–2011, it's 10.05%, close to our guess.

In 2009, the market's annual return was 26.46%.

In 2010, it was 8%.

Dennis M. Wilson

So, you can see even for us to GUESS at returns in the real world, it would be about timing and which fund you selected.

If we redid our spreadsheet to include a simple 10% annual compounded daily increase in bitcoin value... What would OUR actual numbers become? In the last two years the increase has been 3 or 4 times this amount so this is a conservative number.

Earned your Money back in 212 days
Earned $2,676.31 in 1 year
Earned $3,486.55 in 2 years
Contract became unprofitable at 3145 days
Total Value including original contract purchase price: $3,812.63

Of course, a TON of variables are estimated or guessed at to create these numbers, but we tried to make it a fairly bad situation based upon CURRENT realities at the time of this article being written in August of 2017.

The Elephant in the Room

Many would say your money is safer in a mutual fund. This would depend on what your mining objectives were. If you took your bitcoin rewards out regularly to USD, and made it past the effective repayment of your original contract, and bitcoin fell to 50% of its value. YOUR initial contract purchase is back in your hands and you are safe. If you gambled and kept it in bitcoin, you would lose.

How about the real world? If you got to $4436.35 in account value and the stock market crashed taking

50% of your investment, you would have LOST your returns, just like if you had held bitcoin.

The crypto mining world goes crazy saying you won't get your investment back for more than 6 months. How does this get made to sound like a terrible thing? The real world is far more unfair with rates of return, management fees, than playing in the Cloud Mining contract space.

Keep in mind, the reason the rewards can be higher, is the RISK is HIGHER. You COULD lose all your money in your mining contract should it become unprofitable. You could also get involved at a time coins a spiking in value and your contracts return money to you FASTER and FASTER, just like if you owned your own mining rig, minus the hassles.

Finding the Best Cloud Mining Company

Cloud mining is not an exact science. Unlike the usual offline and online businesses where everything is set in writing, cloud mining has far too many variables that can affect potential earnings and as such it is almost unpredictable. In some ways, it resembles stock trading because of the risks associated.

To minimize losses, and profit more in cloud mining, cloud miners make calculated risks by checking on the following when looking for a cloud mining site.

❑ **Credibility** – Since most cloud mining companies never reveal the exact location of their cloud mining facilities, the only way to establish a site's credibility is to do extensive internet research on the company. Some of the best indicators you are dealing with a legit cloud mining company are its age and size. Companies 3 years and older are more likely to be legit since most ponzi schemes do not last that long (one exception was Bernard Madoff's investment scam that lasted 18 years undetected). Another indicator is the size of its customer base. In this case, the larger the customer base, the better (strength in numbers). However, size is not entirely foolproof so you want to research in depth reading with the education you have in this course so you can decipher sour grapes vs. someone who actually lost money to a scam.

❑ **Track record** – Cloud mining sites seldom reveal their actual payouts but would only tell you their site is payment verified, plus an estimate on how much you'll earn for a specific amount of hash rate on a certain type of currency. In other words, the site is telling you people are indeed getting paid for their mining services. But you still have to take their word with a grain of salt, so always look for user and customer reviews to verify claims. Some cloud miners post detailed reviews of these cloud mining sites on YouTube and cloud mining forums. Caution here though, many do that just to get you their referral ID so they can earn a little money or hashpower should you decide to join cloud mining.

❑ **Mined Currencies** – Although major currencies like Bitcoin and Ethereum are currently the highest in terms of USD value, they're not always the most profitable to mine nowadays, at least not directly. Altcoins are often still your best option when it comes to profitable cloud mining. Preferably, you want to go for sites that have a wide range of minor currencies to choose from. Once you get more experience mining and trading these coins, you'll begin to have a sense of appreciation on having as many minor currencies to choose from instead of just staying on one specific type. It is also important to note, you will find bitcoin payouts that are actually just auto converted alt coin contracts, in which case they are paying the relative same amount as the altcoin contract directly would, just in bitcoin.

❑ **Fees and Contract Price** – You'll quickly notice by looking at different cloud mining sites that maintenance fees and contract prices vary from one company to another. Some factors having an effect on potential earnings are energy consumption and the cost of electricity. In some countries, the cost of electricity is amazingly cheap, and the weather is ideal for mining (cooler climates need less power for cooling systems). Whenever possible, look for cloud mining companies with more affordable hash rates, somewhere around 5 to 20 cents per gigahash. Anything higher or lower, you might want to try it first with a small amount and see if it pays out.

❑ **Auto features** – Some miners love if they can maximize their profits while mining on autopilot. Auto features allow miners to simply 'set and forget' and collect their profits at month or year's end. These features include switching from different pools and different currencies, and trading altcoins at a specific time, hash rate, and value along with other set of parameters determined by the user.

❑ **Amalgamated or Solo** - a new breed of cloud mining company is emerging, kind of like a more secure, insured type of mining operation. They re-sell multiple established companies mining contracts, mixed in with their own mining rigs in a pool. This allows their users to hedge the risk they accidentally put their money into a ponzi scheme that looked good but ultimately disappeared. In an Amalgamated scenario, their overall return would go down, but they would not lose everything. These types of Mining companies do charge slightly higher fees for the security they offer.

Determining Cloud Mining's Profitability

Breaking even can take longer in cloud mining because your earnings come in a constant small trickle vs. having a huge reward from a solo miner you own in a pool. With cloud mining, you're using the hashpower generated by the mining companies mining rigs to mine currencies in a pool (some cloud mining services support multi-pool mining). You are essentially pool mining except you are doing it on other people's hardware, and paying them a maintenance fee for the privilege.

Cloud mining is not linear when it comes to earnings. Over time, a currency's value may rise, fall, spike or plunge unexpectedly. Successful cloud miners have a bit of a 'sixth sense' when it comes to a currency's value. As you get more involved in cryptocurrency mining and are up to date on the latest trends, you'll begin to acquire a gut feeling on which currency will be more profitable to mine or trade with. As the old saying goes, "Never put all your eggs in one basket." Watch your earnings and your currencies all the time.

Cloud mining returns WILL DEGRADE over time. As difficulty increases, should the value of the coin you are mining NOT increase more than the difficulty, the return will slowly decrease to zero.

It is possible to have contracts terminated by cloud mining sites if the contract becomes unprofitable for a stated period of time. Depending on the cloud mining company you are using this varies from 3 days to 60 days. They do so with good reason. Since mining requires energy consumption, if your chosen currency or your hash rate for that currency is insufficient to produce net income, the cloud mining company will opt to terminate the contract to avoid a further loss revenue by paying for a mining rig that is not earning more than its maintenance and electricity costs. Once again, keep an eye on your earnings and monitor the trends.

Comparison of Cloud Mining Companies

Here is a comparison of well-known cloud mining companies regarding fees, contract prices, and payouts. (Note: values given here WILL change over time, please not the published date on this document shown on the 2nd page)

Genesis Mining

A trusted and well-known, top-of-mind company in cloud mining. Almost every cryptocurrency miner you bump into knows this company and likely started in the beginning with a contract with them. They mine various currencies that use SHA 256, Ethash, and X11. Starting price is USD 30 for 200 GH/s, depending on the type of currency and hash algorithm.

<u>www.genesis-mining.com</u>

Hashing24

Also a well-known cloud mining site, suspended its affiliate program due to limited amounts of BitFury mining capacity for it to resell. They also run out of hashpower to sell reasonably regularly and suspend sales entirely. Its pricing structure is also laid out very clearly and is based on bitcoin so fluctuates wildly in terms of USD or any Fiat currency. With current Bitcoin prices, it makes their contracts almost 2x as expensive as others and therefore their $return/$spent is the lowest of any providers we monitor as of this time.

As of the moment, their lowest contract price is $26.95 USD for 100/GH/s. As a result, their return per $ spent on a contract is one of the lowest due to the extreme jump in bitcoins price recently. The other drawback is there is not an option to choose which pool to mine your currencies.

https://www.hashing24.com

Hashflare

An emerging competitor amongst top cloud mining service providers. Hashflare supports as many as 5 hash algorithms including Scrypt and Equihash in addition to the more popular SHA 256, Ethash, and X11. They also offer 10% referral bonuses, and multi-pool mining and auto re-invest features. Users can get 10GH/s for USD $1.20. This depends on the currency and hash algorithm you plan to mine. Mining Litecoin, for instance, is priced USD 8.20 1MH/s.

https://hashflare.io

Mining Solutions for PCs and Laptops Altcoin Pool Miners

Mining with PCs and laptops for major currencies has already reached a dead end. Back in the day, Bitcoin, valued at only USD 13.00 by 2012, could be mined with just an average home PC or laptop.

Fast forward 2017, Bitcoin's value ballooned to a staggering USD $4,200.00 with hash rates of nearly 8EH/s! Miners can only dream of 2009 when Bitcoin was largely ignored by most people. Unfortunately, there's no going back to the old days, and it will only get harder to mine in years to come.

So how exactly can our PCs and laptops be feasible for mining in this day and age? The solution is not of brute strength in terms of hashing power but of finesse and a little bit of luck.

Mining Pools

In the early days of cryptocurrency mining, each miner has his own copy of a complete blockchain ledger. Miners are essentially functioning as full nodes, which not only mines blocks, but helps validate the blocks and update the whole network as well.

As blockchains increased in size and the difficulty of each block required higher hash rates, maintaining a complete ledger for validating transactions started to take its toll on their bandwidth and mining capability. Bitcoin nodes, for instance, requires a whopping 150

GB of space to maintain a complete blockchain ledger!

(source: https://bitinfocharts.com)

This fact led to the creation of a different mining approach which has the 'nodes' and the 'miners' working together instead of doing all the work by themselves. The mining community came up with a clever solution that would enable them to participate in mining and still be able to profit from it.

They realized that if they would band together and pool their resources in solving that one particular block of transaction, they would still be able to make something out of their limited mining tools. Miners working together by the thousands in mining pools won't have to maintain individual copies of the complete blockchain ledger; the pool servers do it for them. In effect, pool servers became the 'nodes' in the cryptocurrency network.

Mining pools were able to put the average miners back into the game. It allowed them to earn just enough from bits and pieces of proof-of-work rewards with increased regularity instead of waiting for uncertain number of days coming up with a solved block. Mining pools should afford small-time PC and laptop miners an ideal mining environment, and for a time, it did so – until the 'big boys' came with their massively powerful ASICs and custom-built mining rigs.

Fortunately, they're not that interested in 'cheap' altcoins since they bought these expensive rigs for hunting big game to get their money back as soon as

Dennis M. Wilson

possible. For PC and laptop miners who didn't have to spend too much on mining, these altcoins provide an alternative small source of residual income.

The Major Shift to Minor Altcoins

Just two years after Bitcoin, altcoins started to propagate across the cryptocurrency world, which included Litecoin, Peercoin, Dogecoin and more. When major currencies reached the Terahash, Petahash, and now, Exahash for Bitcoin, miners started to shift to low-priced, but still mineable altcoins because of their relatively low hash rates.

Choosing the Right PC or Laptop for Pool Mining

It should be very clear from the outset that the main purpose of acquiring a PC or laptop is not solely for cryptocurrency mining but for other reasons such as gaming, entertainment, or productivity. Mining should only be during idle hours or periods of inactivity and not as a full-time endeavor, since PCs and laptops are not ideally suited for mining (you'll toast them soon enough if you do).

CPUs won't do so much when it comes to hashpower; GPUs do. If you have a Core i5 PC, you just need a good GPU to run the mining software. Some will try to overclock their GPUs to increase hashpower. You may also do some tweaks, but do so at your own risk. Remember, higher hash rates equals more heat which often equates to shorter life and additional running cost on maintenance and electricity.

Gaming laptops with one or two GPUs are excellent for mining altcoins in a pool. Whenever possible, find something that has an efficient heat management feature to protect your device. Top-of-the-line GPUs are especially important when choosing your laptop since they will do most of the heavy lifting when solving blocks with other miners in a pool.

Ideally, you need around 25 to 50 GH/s to see some results mining with your PC or laptop based on the current hash rates of most minor altcoins (note: values may vary over time. See https://bitinfocharts.com for more). AMD and Nvidia are the industry leaders when it comes to GPUs. Most high-end laptops come with one of these manufacturers GPU. For a detailed comparison of GPUs and their hashing power, you can check:

https://en.bitcoin.it/wiki/Non-specialized_hardware_comparison

Some GPUs can reach up to 670 MH/s (ATI 6990) while most brands are just within the 25 GH/s range (overclocking may slightly increase hash rate).

When using your own PC, you'll have the advantage of being able to use as many as 6 GPUs as opposed to just having 2 with most high-end laptops. Your GPU's can withstand more heat if you take the case panels off or place them in a custom-built frame. However, by doing so, you will have invested a lot of money and you'll be using a lot of power as you have essentially just turned your PC into a GPU mining rig).

Keep Tabs on Minor Altcoins for Profitability

Dennis M. Wilson

When joining pools, always look for ones that include minor altcoins which are capable of being mined by your device and have the potential of going up in value. Some altcoins that were once minable by small-time miners such as Litecoin (LTC), Dash, Dogecoin (DOGE), have already gone up in terms of hash rates while Monero (XMR), and Zcash (ZEC) are still within reach at the time of writing.

There are more than 900 cryptocurrencies on the Internet as of July 2017 (and counting). To profit mining these altcoins, it takes some research and a little luck to forecast the probability of an altcoin going up in value, after which you may choose to keep them, or trade them for Bitcoins or Ethereum.

The rule of thumb is you should always "buy low, sell high." In other words, you need to be able to wait for the opportune time for your altcoins value to grow just enough compared to your target currency to give you a profit. Or, you may choose to have your payouts in Bitcoins or Ethereum right away.

Mine Safely

PCs are more robust than laptops and can withstand more mining abuse. Laptops, on the other hand, can literally melt down and catch on fire when used solely for mining particularly with major, hard-to-mine altcoins.

It's not worth risking running the machine at overclocked settings 24/7 for just a tiny fraction of a reward from mining pools.

Popular Mining Pools

For the blockchain and crypto currencies to stay distributed it is important to not let any particular mining pool or country of mining pools get too powerful. Right now things are heavily slanted to China's amazing power in mining pools, for the sake of balance CryptEdu.com recommends going with a country other than China for your mining pool until the balance is a bit better distributed over the world.

Non-China
Slushpool.com
China
https://pool.btc.com

AFTER you Have Successfully Mined Coins?

One of the first things you need to do once you get a mining contract, or a rig operating, is get yourself set up with an exchange and some crypto wallets.

What is a Cryptocurrency Exchange?

Cryptocurrency Exchanges are websites that allow you to buy, or sell or exchange cryptocurrencies and also usually give you a simple to use wallet.

Exchanges are your key to purchasing crypto currency like Bitcoin and Ethereum should your cloud mining company or mining rig provider only accept crypto currency as a payment method.

Exchanges also are where you can have your various crypto currency wallets to have your mining profits transferred into.

You will need a different wallet for each cryptocurrency you are mining.

CryptEdu.com does NOT support hiding or not paying taxes, so we do NOT support exchanges that do not do follow proper KYC (know your customer) procedures.

Types of Crypto Currency Exchanges

There are generally 3 types of crypto currency exchanges you can be involved with.

Trading Platform

Websites that connect buyers and sellers of cryptocurrency and charge a nominal fee on each transaction.

Direct Trading Platform

A platform that allows you to put up YOUR cryptocurrency at any price you feel you are willing to accept, or hopeful to receive. These direct trading exchanges do not have a set fee, you set your own fee.

Brokerages

Websites anybody can visit to purchase cryptocurrencies at a price set by the broker. The exchange takes a fee.

Exchange Fees

There are generally 3 different ways exchanges make money relating to fees.

The first is, they often charge for you to put money into your account depending on yoru payment method. They often offer some FREE methods that take a while to process, and faster options for a fee. Many accept Visa/Mastercard for smaller amounts but surcharge it sometimes as much as 10%.

The second is a tiny transaction fee on every "TRADE" of one currency to another if you are dealing with an exchange that supports this.

The third is a fee for withdrawal. This again is often done in way that a withdrawal method that takes 7 to 10 days will be FREE or very inexpensive, vs. a method that is faster will be heavily surcharged.

Don't get angry at an exchange because they charge you for their service. They are companies and they need to earn a profit to keep the exchange alive, safe and secure. If they don't, YOUR CRYPTO CURRENCY BALANCE with them would be at RISK.

Before Signing up to an Exchange

As the cryptocurrency world is all relatively new, it is full of new companies. As a result it is not always easy to tell the difference between a big player, a small less stable player, and an outright scam.

Doing your due diligence should include the research on the following.

Payment Methods Accepted

What payment types are accepted to buy crypto currency and what are the limits to each method? Visa? Mastercard? Other Credit/Debit cards? Paypal? Wire Transfer? Make sure you select an exchange with payment IN and payment OUT methods you can live with. Credit cards will be heavily surcharged and require full KYC to be used due to chargeback risk to the exchange. Wire transfers take time as a result of the antiquated centralized banking system the cryptocurrency world is poised to replace.

Reputation of Exchange

Some Google work is required here. Google words like Your target exchange name and the word scam. The same thing and the word fraud added instead of scam. Search for real user reviews, but be careful it is not a review written with a referral link in it as it may not be there for any reason other than to earn that person referral commissions. Forums like

"BitcoinTalk" and "Reddit" can also be helpful in establishing if an exchange is worthy of your future crypto currency fortunes.

Exchange Fees

Remember, there are 3 types of fees. Make sure you understand them clearly and more importantly that you can find them clearly disclosed on your target exchanges website. These fees vary wildly, so you may find yourself joining 2 or 3 exchanges to access the best of all worlds.

KYC (know your customer) Requirements

As we at CryptEdu.com do NOT support hiding or not paying taxes, this is simple advice. Choose an exchange that is legitimate and requires you to not be in hiding. This will help you not be perceived as a criminal or tax evader by your government. We also highly recommend paying taxes on your gains and income properly to the letter of your countries laws.

Often the process of KYC includes you uploading a recent picture of yourself holding your driver's license or passport and a piece of paper with the exchanges name and current date on it. Some go further to insist on a utility bill or bank statement to verify your address as well. The more verification required the more likely an exchange is legitimate and the safer your funds are as they will NOT attract the criminal element.

Countries Serviced

As a result of KYC and legal requirements specific to countries, most legitimate exchanges do NOT service all countries. Many do allow you to purchase bitcoin and other crypto currencies as well as send crypto currency to anybody else anywhere in the world, but do NOT allow withdrawals unless they have all legal documents in YOUR country in order to avoid money laundering allegations and legal action.

Exchange Rates

Watch your exchange rates carefully! Look at a few different exchanges as the rates fluctuate dramatically between exchanges. Always balance great rates with reputation though. Rates can be 10% or more different between exchanges.

Cryptocurrency Exchange Listing

USA
Coinbase

Coinbase is likely the largest and most well known in the world. It has significant investor backing and is recognized as a leader. The one caution is they do NOT allow withdrawals in all countries, for example you cannot withdraw money if you are a Canadian citizen among others.

https://www.coinbase.com

Poloniex

Poloniex handles a lot of currency types and really works as a platform for day traders and active traders more than a simple buy and sell bitcoin type of an exchange.

https://poloniex.com

Canada
Coinpayments.net handles multiple currencies and has a great interface for merchants as well.

https://www.coinpayments.net

Quadrigacx

Dennis M. Wilson

Quadrigacx is a Canadian exchange that services deposits and withdrawals to Canadian citizens by wire transfer, Interac payment amongst others.

https://www.quadrigacx.com

Cryptocurrency Debit Cards

Cryptocurrency debit cards have really started to take off. There are a few things to be cautious of when deciding to get one. We suggest the first is to NOT trust a huge balance to the card issuer, or the third party that is allowing you to fund your card.

How They Work

The way the cryptocurrency debit cards generally work is, you join a company that offers a card, it is often NOT their card, rather they are a client of the card issuer.

You transfer your bitcoin to the CARD SELLER and the bitcoin wallet they will create for you there. Then you will transfer your money from that wallet to your debit card.

Once the money is on the debit card, it is technically at risk Whether your bitcoin balance is or not is dependent upon the structure of the CARD SELLER.

The reason the money you put on your card becomes at risk is your funds will be in a shared account that belongs to the CARD SELLER but controlled by the CARD ISSUER.

Should the company you bought your card from (CARD SELLER) end up in some legal issues with any single one of their card holders, their entire account can be frozen by the CARD ISSUER, meaning YOUR MONEY also becomes unavailable due to this freeze, which was beyond your control, and often even beyond the control of the CARD ISSUER.

We advise just for peace of mind to not transfer to a spendable balance of fiat currency any more than you plan to withdraw or spend within the next 24 hours.

Dennis M. Wilson

Here are some cryptocurrency debit cards worth looking at.

Cryptopay.com

MLM Crypto Currency Mining

Sadly, there are a lot of SCAMS out there in the MLM Crypto Currency marketplace.

Once simple way to know you should steer clear is if they offer any GUARANTEED daily return. If it sounds to good to be true, as you can agree from the knowledge you have gained from this living book, IT LIKELY IS!

NO, a GUARANTEED 1% per day return is NOT possible forever, it may not even be that realistic for a day or two. Even if it was possible once in a while, it will for sure NOT be daily and it will for sure NOT last as per the fact the mining difficulty will keep going up and up.

Also, be suspect of any MLM saying they are doing their OWN mining. This would mean should the MLM you have joined decide to stop operating or go out of business or get attacked by the regulators, YOU WOULD LOSE YOUR CONTRACT.

Look for MLM's that are reselling reputable companies' contracts and you are getting access to those contracts OUTSIDE the MLM Software as well as a possible passthrough.

Here is a list of clients of our associated companies re-selling CryptMin.com contracts and CryptEdu.com Living Books.

http://www.digitalgoldshare.com/

What is a Living Book?

As the cryptocurrency space is changing so rapidly, almost any book you buy, or website or blog post you read will be out of date by the time you read it.

The Living Book Concept will help to over come this. Once you buy our Living book license, every time we have an update to it, you will get an email, or notification if you have downloaded our Living Book App announcing the newest version.

The newest version will always have a different color of text for any information changed since the last version so you can rapidly get up to speed on what changed.

You also have the ability in your living book back office to adjust ALL the affiliate links used throughout the book to be your own.

This allows you to share information with people you care about, and they share your love of Cryptocurrency and act on any links in the book, you will receive credit.

The book is NOT FREE, but can be FREELY SHARED with those you care about or you think will be interested. They only pay for it if they like it and feel it gave them value or would like to participate in the Affiliate Link portion of the book before they share it.

Should you want to, you can also take part in the CryptEDU.com Affiliate program and earn from anybody who decides to license the book after reading your copy.

We always welcome your feedback, ideas for new sections, and arguments to what is written. We expect this book to grow from our research and community feedback to become the de-facto bible on all things related to Cryptocurrency mining.

Proof

Made in the USA
Columbia, SC
03 September 2017